T0196823

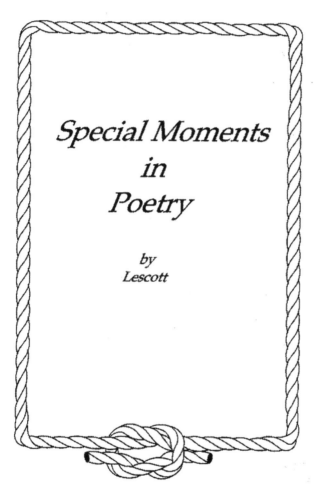

# Special Moments
# in
# Poetry

*by*
*Lescott*

Written and Illustrated by Lescott

Order this book online at www.trafford.com
or email orders@trafford.com

Most Trafford titles are also available at major online book retailers.

Print information available on the last page.

ISBN: 978-1-4120-8775-9 (sc)

*Trafford rev. 11/20/2018*

 www.trafford.com
**North America & international**
toll-free: 1 888 232 4444 (USA & Canada)
fax: 812 355 4082

## Dedication

*I dedicate this to all with whom I have crossed paths in my life – those who have inspired me, influenced me, encouraged me, and become a part of who I am.*

Within these pages lies a compilation of selected poems from nearly five decades of writing. Some very personal moments of struggle and triumph, some whimsical moments, some romantic and some spiritual, mixed with patriotic and introspective… addressing feelings of navy life, romance, marriage, life and death, it is a brave attempt to share thoughts that that could not be shared in any other way.

I hope it will prompt a smile, a tear or spur a look at your own memories and dreams..

### Sometimes

*Sometimes at night,*
*when all is still,*
*I get up from my bed.*
*I tiptoe to a quiet spot,*
*and empty out my head.*
*I write it all on paper -*
*the thoughts and things I feel;*
*'til when at last, my mind is clear,*
*back to my bed I steal.*

## Know

*A man cannot write down of love*
*unless tis in his heart.*
*A man cannot expect to tell*
*or otherwise impart*
*a feeling, hope, joy, hate, or pain*
*or emotion from the soul.*
*He must have first experienced it*
*before it can be told.*

## Poetry

*Poetry, like music*
*comes from near the heart.*
*It flows, - it isn't written,*
*and emotion prompts its start.*
*To call it work or labor*
*just wouldn't tell it right;*
*tho' oft it begs commitment*
*of hours day or night.*
*For it cannot be just dribbled*
*like ink from out the pen,*
*but rather deftly woven*
*like all tapestries of men.*
*It bubbles like a fountain*
*and splashes to and fro,*
*relating thoughts and feelings*
*as onward it must flow.*
*Until what must be spoken*
*has had its place and time;*
*not another word is needed,*
*but wait – just one more line….?*

*So, one thought brings another*
*and a new poem is begun.*
*Sometimes it seems unending.*
*Ah, the love is never done.*

## The Smile

*Someone special came my way*
*when I was in an awful day.*

*She just appeared without a warning*
*when it had been a dreadful morning.*

*In she came, and said hello…*
*Why she came, I still don't know.*

*I was set to feel so bad.*
*I had it made up to be sad.*

*But in she came, with smile so sweet,*
*freckled cheeks, and two bare feet.*

*Her hair all tousled round her face,*
*In my lap she took her place.*

*She said "Daddy, I love you!"*
*I said, of course, "I love you too."*

*We chatted for a while and then,*
*I looked, and she was gone again.*

*But in my room, she left her smile.*
*I think I'll keep it for a while.*

## A Friend

*We were friends right from the start*
*as he reached out for my hand;*
*and with that friendly open grin*
*I knew he'd understand.*
*Tho' our friendship was a brief one,*
*he was a Pastor with a heart,*
*who knew my need of family*
*- and with his I become a part.*
*He shared his family, meals and home*
*with a sailor in need of friends,*
*making me always feel welcome,*
*knowing I may not pass this way again.*
*I never hesitated for a moment*
*to feel at ease with him.*
*For if I paused to think of words*
*he'd encourage with a grin.*
*We often walked and worked and played*
*- the feeling never changed.*
*For when I was low, he cheered me up*
*- my whole life re-arranged.*
*And when we parted - all too soon,*
*there was no sad good-bye.*
*For when you've known such Christian love,*
*there's no need for tearful eye.*
*I often feel an empty place*
*down somewhere in my heart,*
*but I remember that friendly grin*
*and feel my own smile start.*

## Suppose...

*Suppose we were friends*
*just you and me*
*Suppose we sat down*
*under a big green tree*
*Would our friendship grow*
*would we laugh and chat*
*would we share secret dreams*
*and all like that*
*Would we watch ripples dance*
*in the water's edge*
*or cloud castles build*
*in the sky overhead*
*Would we pick blades of grass*
*and tickle for fun*
*or seriously watch*
*a late setting sun*
*You can never be sure*
*just what we would do*
*til after it's over*
*and that door you've gone through*
*But of this I'm sure -*
*I think you'll agree*
*we'd be special friends*
*- just you and me.*

## Special Friends

*Our hearts were joined together*
*in friendship pure and true.*
*We shared our many problems*
*as I bared my heart to you.*
*We found the truest meaning*
*of companionship and love.*
*We pleaded for the guidance*
*of heaven up above.*
*Our hearts were quick to hunger*
*for the things that could not be;*
*but we found by heavenly wisdom*
*a better way, you see.*
*We found the joy of loving*
*in a way few people know.*
*We are happy in the knowledge*
*of heavenly friendship down below.*

*We shared our many problems,*
*and oh, the peace we found,*
*as our hungry hearts sought sympathy*
*where compassion did abound.*
*So you have become a part of me*
*and ne'er will I forget,*
*the thoughts we shared together*
*since the first day that we met .*
*May this love and friendship linger*
*through all the days ahead.*
*May it strengthen and encourage you*
*when'er sad words are said.*

# Friendship

*We met and for a moment*
*our hearts were in accord.*
*You shared with me your problems.*
*I devoured ever word.*
*And then we turned the tables*
*while I told you of me.*
*You, too, were a good listener;*
*you proved a friend to be.*

*Now friendship is not something*
*you use and throw away.*
*Neither is it but a word*
*forgotten in a day.*
*It is the act of being loved*
*and loving in return -*
*to really care and give and share*
*with genuine concern.*

*Now we have made this union*
*and forever friends will be .*
*by your giving, taking ,sharing,*
*you've become a part of me.*
*Tho' you may have never realized -*
*it's sometimes very slight -*
*you've made a difference in my life*
*by word or deed that was just right.*

*Like ships exchanging cargo -*
*each seldom changes weight.*
*They never change their outward look,*
*yet they change each other's fate.*

*For they'll never be again the same*
*and when in time they part,*
*they'll carry something of the other*
*deep within their heart.*

### Tokens

*You never asked for gifts*
*I didn't promise any*
*You didn't ask for spending*
*(I seldom have a penny)*
*But when I bring a token*
*no matter what the size*
*to let you know you're thought about*
*there's something in your eyes*
*that lets me know I wasn't wrong*
*you understand and care*
*And then I wish - I really wish*
*I had much more to share*

## Words

*If I could only write the words*
*I think about today;*
*I'd tell how I love you*
*- in every silly way.*
*I'd write about our special times,*
*and very secret dreams.*
*I'd write the long and mixed-up words*
*of complicated schemes.*
*I'd write of tender moments*
*I'll cherish in my heart.*
*But if a wrote a million words,*
*it would only be a start.*

## Our Song

*If i had my way*
*every moment with you*
*would linger forever*
*every dream would come true*
*every tear would bring laughter*
*every heartache bring joy*
*if I had my way*

*If I had my way*
*every sunset would be*
*painted with crimson*
*and you'd view it with me*
*Every sunrise I'd wake*
*To find you by my side*
*if I had my way*

*I would wish for you blue skies*
*and gardens of flowers*
*I would sing to you softly*
*for hours and hours*
*We'd dance in the moonlight*
*and never grow tired*
*If I had my way*

## My fair Companion

*God gave us all the beauty*
*of earth and sky and sea.*
*He gave us all this beauty*
*to hear and feel and see.*

*But then He gave one more thing*
*to make our lives complete.*
*He gave hearts of feeling*
*and to love He did entreat.*

*He gave us fair companions*
*to cherish and to hold.*
*Ah, this is beauty at its best...*
*a love that won't grow cold.*

*You are my fair companion.*
*You are so dear to me.*
*You are the beauty of my heart,*
*and this you'll always be.*

### The Picture

*She watches through her window*
*my every move and mood.*
*She smiles the same sweet smile*
*- even when I'm rude.*
*She's traveled with me many miles*
*o'er calm and stormy sea.*
*and every time I look up,*
*she's  smiling down at me.*
*I know the features of her face*
*I see them with eyes closed.*
*Her watching eyes are before me still*
*when I drift into sweet repose.*
*She tells me that she loves me,*
*tho' she never says a word.*
*The silence of her smiling face*
*says things that can't be heard.*
*We'll always be together*
*o'er calm and stormy sea;*
*and every time I look up*
*she'll be smiling down at me.*

### The Fiftieth Year

*Fifty years -*
*so quickly gone*
*since we said those words*
*and vowed to be one.*
*The years spent in dreaming*
*and building our home*
*sharing and caring*
*- never alone...*

*It seems only yesterday,*
*when we were so young,*
*never giving a thought*
*that this day would come.*
*But young we still are*
*in our heart, don't you see,*
*and I care for you*
*as you care for me.*

*Fonder and fonder*
*each moment we grow,*
*and onward and onward*
*through life we will go.*

## Together

*As the sky grows dark around us*
*And the dew begins to fall*
*As the stars begin to twinkle*
*And the night birds make their call*

*I reach to draw you closer*
*And I feel your warm embrace*
*I feel your whispered breathing*
*Warm and sweet against my face*

*I hear your gentle murmur*
*As contentment we do share*
*In the dark'ning evening shadows*
*It is good to know you're there.*

## Fantasy

*I woke this morn and you were gone*
*- Or were you ever there?*
*I'd dreamed a dream of fantasy*
*It was a dream so fair*
*We danced and sang as lovers*
*We talked into the night*
*We kissed with sweetest kisses*
*Until the morning light*
*Then I awoke and silly me*
*I'm where I've always been*
*But how I love my dream of you*
*We'll meet, and dance again.*

## Make-Believe

*Surely there is a place for folk like me*
*who live in make-believe.*
*Surely there is use for us*
*who troubled paths do weave.*
*We live in lives of fantasy*
*and wish for silver clouds.*
*but when the world comes crashing down,*
*we're annoyed by the sound.*

# Tree house

*I climbed up in the tree house;*
*it was a lovely day.*
*I settled in and sat a while*
*in such a childish way.*

*My bare feet dangled o'er the side;*
*the sun shone on my head.*
*"It's nice to be a boy again",*
*my boyish inside said.*

*And so I sat in summer sun*
*and dreamed of yesteryear.*
*Rememb'ring days so long ago*
*when I longed to be here.*

*Remembering how I used to dream*
*of one day being tall,*
*and have a home and family*
*thinking then I'd have it all.*

*I haven't changed at all, I tho't ,*
*except that now I'm tall.*
*Inside there's still that little boy*
*who dreams to have it all.*

*And safe up in the tree house,*
*with the world spread out below,*
*I can dream of anything*
*and only God will know.*

*The leafy branches overhead*
*swayed in the summer breeze*
*as chirping birds extolled their joy*
*to share with me their trees.*

*In the land of make-believe,*
*we dare not linger long.*
*So I returned again to earth*
*But I kept the robin's song*

## Take Me Back to Make-Believe

*Take me back to make-believe*
*Where things are always fair*
*Where there never is a problem*
*And never is a care*

*Where the sun is always shining*
*And the sky is always blue*
*Take me back to make-believe*
*Let me spend a day with you*

*We'll visit many castles*
*And ride on prancing steeds*
*Wearing shining armor*
*Doing many wondrous deeds*

*We'll sing the greatest operas*
*And bow for the applause*
*We'll perform before the king and queen*
*Taking nothing – just because…*

*We will be forever young there*
*Playing, laughing, having fun*
*And go to sleep on feather beds*
*When our make believe is done*

### Fireflies

*As fireflies go darting*
*Amidst the summer skies*
*And children chase them laughing*
*With excitement in their eyes*
*The darkness slowly falling*
*Brings with its eerie light*
*A shroud of friendly mystery*
*About the coming night.*

*The fireflies are here then there*
*A blink and then a glow*
*They light their pathway from behind*
*-where they've been , not where they'll go*

## Evening

*There comes a time*
*at the end of the day,*
*when toil is ended*
*and so is the play.*
*The lamps are lit*
*as we all gather in*
*for supper and chatter*
*to tell where we've been.*
*The chores are all finished.*
*There's now time to rest*
*in the warmth of the family*
*like a warm, cozy, nest.*
*We bring to a close,*
*like the page of a book,*
*this chapter of life*
*and the time that it took.*
*The hustle and bustle*
*and sounds of the day*
*like the heat of the sunshine*
*have drifted away.*
*Soon comes the darkness*
*and peace that it brings*
*as over each pillow*
*a lullaby sings.*
*A long peaceful slumber*
*will be the next goal -*
*rest for the body,*
*and rest for the soul*

## Dawn

As the first grey shadows lighten
into misty morning light,
the day takes shape before me;
forgotten is the night.
The brightness of a shining moon
fades to a pale white dim.
The black beyond begins to turn
into a blue again.
And as the wind-tossed branches
brush away the morning mist,
each leaf shakes off the memory
of last evening's dewy kiss.
The morning dove begins her song
- a gentle cooing sound.
The other songbirds enter in
- a chorus all around.
And as in lofty serenade,
the birds announce the sun,
she wakens with her stretching rays
- her warmth has just begun.
She reaches to the shadows,
and the darkness runs away.
And once again in nature's plan
the world begins another day.

# The Autumn Leaf

*Every autumn leaf that falls,*
*Drifting to the ground...*
*leaves its lofty summer place*
*to rest without a sound.*
*Where once it hung a verdant green,*
*enjoying summer breeze;*
*It now will lie forgotten,*
*beneath the barren trees.*
*In a final reach for glory*
*it turns all red and gold*
*and rustles faintly to be heard*
*- a struggle, oh so bold.*
*But then, alas, it's over;*
*it lies in sweet repose.*
*It lies with many others*
*awaiting winter snows.*

## The Garden

Beneath the dark, foreboding skies
in autumn's chilly breeze,
Lies the garden, stark and cold,
o'er hung by barren trees.
Where once hung fruit and bounteous crop,
there now are empty vines
and where the brightest flowers swayed
dry stalks lie intertwined.
But in the center, like a tomb,
- a neatly structured mound . . .
Autumn's leaves, like nature's quilt
tell of treasure underground
Beneath the leaves, life yet remains
protected from the cold
Like pirate's treasure buried there
a row of nature's gold
- golden carrots, still in bed
will sleep in winter's night,
and waken on a table warm
for that delicious bite.

## December Morn

*I woke this morn before the dawn*
*and rose to meet the day.*
*I pushed aside the curtain wide*
*to see what'er I may.*

*Such a view, I've seldom known.*
*I tho't perhaps a dream -*
*for on the lawn, winter'd come,*
*and left a Christmas scene.*
*The lawn had now a coverlet,*
*where last bare grass I'd seen;*
*and every branch and twiglet*
*was dressed all white and clean.*
*Each post now wore a little cap*
*- the flagpole did as well,*
*And now just where the street began*
*it was quite hard to tell.*

*I hurried with my winter clothes*
*- my mittens, boots, and coat,*
*to be a part of wonderland*
*- ev'ry picture there to note.*
*Then with the shovel I did start*
*to carve my path of sorts,*
*and push my way along the drive*
*to view God's handiwork.*

## Spectators

*Did you ever watch the sea and sky*
*and wonder where they met?*
*Did you ever contemplate on life*
*til' many long hours you'd spent?*

*How God could make a world so vast*
*in all His tender love -*
*and every rainbow in the sky*
*He has painted from above?*

*It takes a wiser man that me*
*to understand the reasons,*
*But it takes a simple man like me*
*to appreciate the seasons.*

*Man can build cathedral tall,*
*with architecture fine,*
*or smash in two the atom small,*
*or probe the human mind.*
*But man can't cause the wind to blow*
*or put leaves on a tree.*
*We only use this earth, you know...*
*We're spectators, you and me.*

# A Meditation

*The sea is still, the sky is dark*
*and onward steams the ship.*
*Twill leave no track, twill leave no mark*
*to tell of the lonely trip.*

*The lookouts stand both fore and aft*
*and watch the sea pass by.*
*They watch for signs of other craft*
*afloat or in the sky.*

*The world is silent save for the groan*
*of the engines down below.*
*we're all alone, our course unknown*
*to others as they go.*

*But in the night one thing is true*
*to those who meditate.*
*Tis only God and His great crew*
*could such an earth create.*

*And as I look up toward the stars*
*I think of heavenly things -*
*of mansions bright and golden streets*
*of angels, robes and kings.*

*I've seen high mountains and rolling plain.*
*I've crossed o'er field and stream,*
*but only here am I so alone*
*with God and His heavenly scheme.*

*He made the sky and made the sea.*
*He keeps them pure and clean*
*- used by man, and viewed by me -*
*I'm led to pray and dream.*

# At Sea

*We sailed for days across the sea,*
*relentless as she was.*
*We sailed for weeks and still no sign*
*of life to cheer our cause.*

*Our course was set for far-off lands*
*no one could turn us back.*
*We churned the water with our screw*
*but left no tell-tale track.*

*The powerful engines groaned and strained*
*beneath their heavy chore;*
*but never faltered in the task*
*to reach that distant shore.*

*By day the crew was hard at work*
*at every well-laid job*
*of chipping paint, making repairs*
*- no leisure could we rob.*

*When darkness fell, the scene was changed*
*while sailors thought of home.*
*They played at games, or read a book*
*or manned a rail alone.*

*Each man was in his own world now*
*where no one could intrude.*
*The darkness hid a tear-filled eye*
*- it covered a solemn mood.*

*And as each man so hard and rough,*
*when working in the light,*

*gave way to feelings all alone*
*became a boy again at night.*

*Each thought of home and loved ones dear*
*that he had left behind,*
*and sought some proper manly way*
*to peace and comfort find.*

*But as I watch the sea and stars*
*as o'er dark decks I trod;*
*I cannot help but feel it there*
*The majesty of God.*

*It's lonely and it's frightening*
*to be at sea at night,*
*but there's comfort in the knowledge*
*that we're always in His sight.*

*I wonder if each honest lad,*
*who's ever sailed the sea,*
*should tell the truth to self and men*
*has felt God just like me.*

# I Wonder

*I often wonder how far it goes -*
*the universe and sky*
*I often wonder why we're here -*
*you as you and I as I*

*I've climbed up to the mountain peak*
*and seen the world below*
*I've looked up from the vale so deep*
*and seen the caps of snow*

*I've crossed the mighty oceans wide*
*and seen her many moods*
*but still my mind cannot quite grasp*
*the greatness of God's goods*

*He formed the mighty mountains*
*He filled the raging sea*
*He placed each star in its own place*
*but left room for you and me*

*He causes rain and sleet and snow*
*He lets the flooding waters flow*
*but when He feels we've had enough*
*He hangs a loving rainbow*

*Up on the mighty mountain's peak*
*down in the vale below*
*Out on the sea, be it wild or still*
*the elements all know*

*The world and all the universe*
*the mountains, sea and sky*
*All are His to rule and reign*
*yet He cares for you and I*

## Divine Services

'Divine Services are being held'
the words ring loud and clear
to some it's a call unwelcome
but to others a call of cheer

The little organ squeaks and sours
the notes are far from right
but to a homesick sailor's voice
it's a fairly even fight

The pulpit's far from perfect,
it's made by layman's hands
but when the book is opened there
a Holy rev'rence stands

The pews are not fine cushioned
they're only mess deck seats
but here you sit and here you pray
when Sunday service meets

As sailors slip into the pews
tho' dressed in dungarees
there is no shown distinction now
you're equal on your knees

The service here is far from homelike
there's no choir or stained glass
but rev'rence reigns and communion's fresh
when the bread and cup are passed

The chaplain does the usual things
you expected him to do
but where the worship really lives
is between your God and you

*You may not agree with the chaplain*
*or belong to his same faith*
*but you don't think of things like that*
*you lose prejudice and hate*

*You're all alone with God at sea*
*to stop and think and pray*
*and if you worship in your heart*
*you need no special words to say*

*The service closes with a hymn*
*'Eternal Father strong to save'*
*you've met and talked and been with Him*
*who fashioned every wave*

*The ship is rolling beneath you*
*the wind is blowing too*
*but far at sea neath the arch of sky*
*God means much more to you.*

# The Mid-Watch

*'Relieve the watch' the word was passed*
*each post was manned anew*
*the clock struck twelve, eight bells rang out*
*to bed went a tired crew*

*The first ten minutes go by fast*
*as you settle at your post*
*But as time ticks on, it slows its pace*
*and it's quiet as a ghost*

*It's half past twelve and you feel an ache*
*in the middle of your back*
*You wish you'd never had to leave*
*that warm and cozy sack.*

*You think that time has stopped for sure*
*when next you check the clock*
*you've stood there for two hours*
*but it's not yet one o'clock*

*You've paced the deck till feet are sore*
*you've read every notice twice*
*you strain your ears to hear some sound*
*if only faint as mice*

*The sea is still and there's no moon*
*the wind is just a whisper -*
*If only you could just sit down*
*- your back is getting stiffer*

*You check the time o'er and again*
*it seems to barely crawl*
*have you been dealt a torture watch*
*where there is no time at all?*

*It's two o'clock - you've made halfway*
*ah, it'll be easy now*
*but where you saw the clock move then*
*no movement now allows*

*Its damp and dark and just a chill*
*to shiver to your bones*
*the morning mist is falling fast*
*to multiply your moans*

*Your arches burn and toes are cold*
*you've a numbness in your knees*
*will someone tell that clock*
*to go a little faster please*

*It's half past two, you start to nod*
*you're sleeping on your feet!*
*with eyes wide open, you're asleep*
*- your misery is complete*

*You hum a song to wake yourself*
*and begin to move about*
*you think about all sorts of things -*
*what life is all about*

*It's three o'clock and almost done*
*you're like a tired machine*
*you make each move by instinct*
*as your aching muscles scream*

*As night turns into morning*
*and darkness turns to grey*
*you wonder if you'll live enough*
*to see the coming day*

*But now it's nearly over*
*and you think of coming rest*
*It wasn't really all that bad*
*now that you've stood the test*

*"the mid-watch, it was easy"*
*to your relief you say*
*"at least I'll get some sleep -*
*you've got a long, long day"*

## A Sailor's Sorrow

*I remember her last smile*
*I remember her last tear*
*I remember how she kissed me*
*and said 'be of good cheer'*

*I tried so not to show it*
*- the way I knew I felt*
*I tried so not to let her see*
*that my heart, too, could melt*

*But we parted there in smiles*
*while underneath we cried*
*and we left each other courage*
*but a little of each died*

*I know she still remembers*
*I know that she still cares*
*I know the joys we cherished*
*she, like me, in mem'ry shares*

*Should I not again see her*
*should we not again embrace*
*should fate forever part us*
*I'll ne'er forget her face*

*But one day soon I'll see her*
*when the war and fighting's o'er*
*One day soon I'm going home*
*and we'll part again no more.*

## The Highway

*The highway stretches on and on*
*like a ribbon through the plain*
*caring not about the tears*
*of the gentle falling rain*
*The endless night, the endless road*
*are melted by the raindrops*
*into a lonely pleasant mood*
*that somehow, too soon stops*

## The Night Bus

*I gaze through glass into the night*
*and see my own reflection*
*tis like a ghost who rides with me*
*to watch my imperfections*
*I smile and wink, it does the same*
*so knowingly and vain*
*We'll be companions through the night*
*- me and my window pane*

## The Open Road

*The open road is more than just*
*a ribbon of concrete.*
*It stretches to another world*
*to make our life complete.*
*We follow like the knight in search*
*of the elusive Holy Grail.*
*Hoping at each turn to find*
*the ending of our trail.*
*And so we cherish each new sight*
*and friend who brings us pleasure.*
*The answer to our quest is found*
*in the search and not the treasure.*


## Golden Gate

*Twas in the early morning,*
*a breeze was in the air.*
*We broke through the tunnel*
*and the Golden Gate was there!*
*She rose so tall before us,*
*where she had stood for years,*
*majestic, overwhelming*
*- it moved a man to tears.*

## Class of Fifty-six

*Hey, Look at us! - Look where we've been,*
*Around the world and back again!*
*Some traveled near – while others went far;*
*But here or there we've followed our star.*
*We said goodbyes and went our way*
*on that, - our graduation day.*
*Then whether to job, or college, or war,*
*we found the niche we were destined for.*
*Some wandered a bit with uncertain ways;*
*others ran to a goal and with it did stay.*
*But for fame or fortune or personal joy,*
*we did what we did – each 'girl' and 'boy'.*
*We were just kids, but look how we've grown!*
*We raised our families and built our homes.*
*We spent all we earned - or socked it away,*
*In anticipation of retirement day.*
*We gave of ourselves to whatever befell;*
*and ran with our hearts to dreams we dreamed well.*

*Look at us now, look how we've changed -*
*the hair we've lost - the weight we've gained.*
*The age spots, the wrinkles, all tell a tale…*
*The dreams that we had are beginning to pale.*
*The dreams that we had in 'fifty-six,*
*are now but faint mem'ries we cannot fix.*
*Look 'round the room - several are gone.*
*One day we'll follow – our time will come.*

*But we'll not go down - we're far from through yet.*
*There's plenty of life in this '56 set.*
*Look at us now you'll see we're still kids,*

*with dreams un-fulfilled and plenty of fizz.*
*Run ahead of our children, ahead of their's too –*
*Show them our stuff and what we can do.*
*And we'll keep coming back tho' older we grow,*
*there's a special bond here that not all can know.*
*"... hail, hail, the gang's all here, round thy colors old*
*we'll stick together for our dear green and gold...."*

### The Reunion

*I entered the room, looking for friends.*
*Not knowing who I might see.*
*I entered the room to see only strangers*
*- they looking strangely at me.*
*I was offered a hand, a smile, and a greeting*
*somebody asked me my name.*
*I mumbled it low as I peered at them cautiously*
*to find they were doing the same.*
*Then slowly emerged the hint of a face,*
*which resembled a friend I once knew.*
*I could tell by the smile that started to break*
*that I had been recognized too!*
*I moved round the room repeating the scene*
*over and over again.*
*This sea of strange faces was no longer strange*
*'twas a room full of long-lost friends!*

*There were hugs and embraces, the room was aglow*
*with chatter and squeals of delight.*
*As laughter resounded, acquaintance renewed,*
*we talked our way into the night.*
*Some settled here, and others there*
*regaling the tales of the past -*
*remembering, sharing, questioning, baring…*
*- Old friends together at last.*

## Lonesome

*My sister went away to school*
*she left her dog behind.*
*My brother went to find a job -*
*some great and special kind.*
*They're both gone and I'm alone.*
*I'm not sure what to do.*
*There's no one now to play with;*
*the house seems, empty too.*
*Mom and Dad stayed on the farm,*
*just like it was the same,*
*but me and Rover can't be still*
*- we feel a funny pain.*
*It's kinda like we're cut inside*
*- I know, of course, we're not.*
*I guess it's cause since they've been gone*
*the weather's been so hot -*
*We check the road for their return*
*- I s'pose they never will,*
*but I could see them far away*
*from up here on this hill.*
*Do you suppose that they don't care?*
*- I mean my mom and Dad.*
*You'd think they'd be here lookin' too*
*(I'd know it if they had).*
*Maybe they just aren't the same*
*as Rover here and me.*
*Maybe it would be too hard for them*
*an empty road to see.*
*I'll have to try to help them more*
*- I mean my Mom and Dad.*
*I'll bet if I should go away,*
*they really would be sad.*

# Old Moley

*Old Moley was a tomcat.*
*He wandered in one day.*
*And tho' quite uninvited,*
*he settled in to stay.*

*With tawny stripes – a handsome coat*
*he resembled jungle kin.*
*He looked us over as to say,*
*"Should I let them take me in?"*

*He killed a mole – hence the name -*
*to let us know he'd work,*
*and react to any little sound*
*with a proper 'hunter's lurk'.*

*One day he sat upon the stoop;*
*the next day just in doors.*
*Then he wandered to the hearth,*
*and claimed a bit of floor.*

*Now he sleeps on Master's bed,*
*or any place he pleases.*
*It seems he's found a home*
*all safe from frosty breezes*

## A Flower

*A flower in the garden*
*helps to make a wondrous hue*
*just a flower - one of many*
*red, yellow, pink or blue*

*A flower plucked and swept away*
*leaves such a vacant spot*
*all others in the garden*
*see only where its not...*

*But when the flower goes away*
*its reached its fullest bloom*
*and now has higher calling*
*to brighten another room.*

## Death's Promise

*We watch the old life wither*
*We watch the dead leaves fall*
*We watch the earth grow dreary*
*We hear the night bird call*

*Soon darkness will be on us*
*Soon summer sunshine gone*
*We'll shiver in the winter*
*And wait for springtime's dawn*

*But in the dark'ning shadows*
*There is one comfort tho't*
*Beneath the slumbering winter*
*The earth, it slumbers not*

*Old life is given to bring new*
*Its giving – not unkind*
*For with the dawn of springtime*
*Comes strength and joy sublime.*

## Fatality

*The wind is cold and heartless*
*as it chills the very soul*
*The moon without expression*
*like the brass atop a pole*
*The trees are all atangle*
*as tho' to fence me in*
*The sky is full of tiny eyes*
*to watch my every sin*
*The ocean goes relentless*
*each wave before the next*
*and I so alone and helpless*
*my very soul is vexed*
*I wonder is life pointless*
*what is the use to live*
*I've tried in vain to live life*
*and to others comfort give*
*I cry to God for mercy*
*I cry for strength and aid*
*I hear no thundering answer*
*I know my bed I've made*
*I know God hears my whisper*
*but the rules have all been laid*
*and once a rule is broken*
*the penalty must be paid*
*I've stepped across a boundary*
*where men should never go*
*I tried to do things my way*
*tho' God's is best I know*
*My heart is torn asunder*
*my mind a weary wreck*
*I feel the fence close in now*

*like icy fingers 'round my neck*
*I've blundered every commission*
*I've done more harm than good*
*There is but one way for me*
*I'd do it if I could...*
*I'd do the world a favor*
*if only I could go...*
*I can't, I must, it's done then -*
*I'll end it all, but, no -*
*What's that on the horizon?*
*the opening of a way?*
*It's the first faint streak of morning*
*- the dawn of another day.*

## Open Window

*Open window to the sky*
*Open window here am I*
*Telling you my private dreams*
*Just to you, my dead soul screams*
*Hear the misery of my plight*
*Hear the sigh of useless flight*

*Open window to the sky*
*Open window here am I*
*Let me see some thin frail light*
*to give me hope on this dark night*
*Give my wretched soul reborn*
*strength to face another morn*

## Purpose

Tonight I wished upon a star
as it streaked across the sky.
Tonight I wished for love and life
as I watched an old world die.
The brightness of that dying star
shone out in a darkened sky.
It gave its light in dying.
must I die to shine? I cry.
I know life has its purpose.
I know we live to shine.
but if there is such purpose,
I ask, I cry, what's mine?

## Thoughts

*I gaze above at summer skies,*
*and see the host of angel eyes.*
*I feel the chill of Satan's whisper,*
*and shiver as a cautious listener.*
*I think of all the worldly things*
*that chilling, tempting, whisper brings...*
*Of love, adventure, sights, and scenes*
*- hot blood goes racing through my veins.*

*The Angel eyes are wisely winking.*
*They know the foolish tho'ts I'm thinking.*
*So far away, they seem to say,*
*'Go on mortal, enjoy your play..*
*Do as you please, enjoy your lusts.*
*We know in time, somehow you must;*
*but remember this, be not deceived,*
*one way is right - you must believe.*
*Your life can last but for a season,*
*and in God's plan each has a reason'*

*The world is such a tiny part -*
*it gives my hope and faith a start.*
*If this is true, and there is hope,*
*why should we madly, blindly grope?*
*Why not use the strength around us -*
*accept the love that sought and found us?*

## Faces

*I study the people I see each day.*
*I watch their faces and what they say.*
*Faces can surely talk - tis so -*
*they let you many secrets know.*
*The lines of sorrow, fear, and hate,*
*I see them there upon the pate.*
*As well as lines of joy and fun*
*with twinkling eyes of the friendly one.*
*And those in love have such a glow...*
*There's oh, so much a face can show.*

## What is an American?

*Go to any country -*
*any spot upon the earth*
*Call together any people -*
*of any size or worth.*
*Take from this the very least -*
*the one with naught to lose;*
*Ask him, then - don't tell him -*
*if he'd like a chance to choose.*
*Let him have a place for choosing -*
*a wilderness so vast*
*that he'll never see the whole of it*
*until his life is past.*
*Let him choose a spot for living;*
*Let him clear away the waste.*
*Let him build and shape his new domain*
*according to his taste.*
*Make it difficult - not easy,*
*through sickness, cold or heat.*
*Let him choose to keep on living,*
*and not admit defeat.*
*Let his wealth be all his making*
*and his health be through his toil.*
*Let him struggle for a living,*
*mid sweat-drops mixed with soil.*
*Let him feel the pain of hatred*
*from prejudice and sin.*
*Let him overcome with courage,*
*letting only justice win.*

*Show him people under burdens -*
*show him some too weak to stand;*
*Let him choose to fight their battles*

*and lend a helping hand.*
*Let him die away from family -*
*'neath another's enemies' sword.*
*Let him choose to die there bravely,*
*believing in his Lord.*
*Oh, he'll worry, moan, and grumble*
*over his poor, unjust plight*
*But he'll struggle on most bravely*
*and revel in the fight.*
*In his heart he'll be contented*
*just choosing to be free*
*and helping those less fortunate*
*a better life to see.*

*Or give him life to fight again*
*some other kind of cause*
*Let him take part in his own way*
*to make or change some laws*
*Let him speak out now most freely*
*of any thought or view,*
*And let him worship where he will*
*in his religion old or new*

*Let him live on for his purpose*
*or have no goal at all*
*This man is one of many -*
*Let him stand alone, and tall.*
*But give him one more choice now*
*Let him stop and look around*
*To survey all the things he's done*
*and what blessings do abound*
*Let him see his many vic'tries -*
*yes, and lack-of-thought mistakes*
*Let him choose if he'll go on,*

*knowing well the price it takes*
*And if he chooses to go on*
*and continue in his stand,*
*your question will be answered -*
*"What is an American?"*
*He'll carry his flag most proudly,*
*always glad to be a part*
*He's more than just a citizen -*
*He's an American in his heart!*

*- DMC Leland R. Scott, USN*
*1971 winner, Freedoms Foundation award*
*and George Washington Medal*

## A Nation Reborn

*A world watched in horror as hatred reigned.*
*It came without warning, a message in flames.*
*Rocking the world with terror and awe,*
*we watched, grief-stricken, the sight that we saw.*
*Consumed in just moments, many lives, many dreams,*
*drowned now by sorrow and anguish and screams.*
*We stood for a moment, stunned by the sight;*
*unable to grasp what foe we must fight.*

*Then out of the ashes and the yet burning flame,*
*sprang the phoenix of courage, of mercy, humane.*
*America stood, reaching out - clasping hands*
*and with her, her friends from every land.*
*We bowed together - together we mourned.*
*Though many lives given, new heroes were born.*

*The plan of terror was foiled that day*
*as nations united to wipe it away.*
*While the ashes still smolder, while the grief lingers on,*
*new anthems are written. New hope marches on.*

*Turning to God for solace and strength,*
*a nation united now stands on the brink*
*of a chapter unwritten in history's tome.*
*America stands to defend freedom's home.*

- 11 September, 2001

# Wait

*The gladdest hearts are sometimes sad.*
*The whitest clouds turn grey.*
*The calmest seas get stormy,*
*and rainbows fade away.*

*For life is never perfect.*
*All days must have a night.*
*But when the battle's failing,*
*don't give up the fight.*

*For somewhere on the horizon*
*another day begins.*
*Somewhere skies are clearing.*
*Somewhere patience wins.*

## Healing

*To a heart once weak and tender*
*To a heart once frail and new*
*To a heart once full of compassion*
*I give these words to you*

*You've suffered grief and sorrow*
*You've felt deep pain and woe*
*You've had cuts too deep for mending*
*but those scars need never show*

*If you'll let the scars bring wisdom*
*If you'll heal the wounds with love*
*If you'll forgive, forget, and trust again*
*you'll find new strength from above.*

## The sun will shine

*When troubles seem too heavy*
*When problems take you down*
*Remember there's a reason*
*And try hard not to frown*
*Just brace up with a smile*
*And turn your thoughts above*
*Just rest upon God's goodness*
*Feel secure in His great love*

*Fill your time with 'busy'*
*Fill your thoughts with cheer*
*Gather those around you*
*Who want to keep you near*
*The darkest cloud will pass away*
*The sun again will shine*
*Perhaps you'll find that grey cloud*
*Is really silver lined.*

### He's There

*Sometimes when life*
*has filled us with care.*
*Sometimes when burdens*
*are too much to bear.*

*Sometimes when pain*
*has brought us to tears.*
*Sometimes when doubt*
*has caused us to fear.*

*Sometimes when we've used*
*all the courage we've known,*
*and circumstances cause us*
*to feel quite alone.*

*There's one thought to warm*
*- one thought to cheer.*
*That thought is the knowledge*
*that Jesus is near.*

*He loves and He cares*
*forever His own.*
*In His arms He enfolds*
*till comfort is known.*

*With the love of a father,*
*there is no greater friend.*
*He never forsakes*
*- love without end.*

### His Plan

*Tonite I talked to God.*
*Tonite I heard Him say,*
*"For you I have a plan*
*Please don't get in the way."*

*He said " I'll show you how".*
*He said "I'll show you when".*
*He said "I will provide -*
*be patient until then."*

### Waiting

*Waiting for the Sunrise*
*waiting for the dawn*
*Waiting for morning*
*with the cheerful robin's song*

*Waiting for the promise*
*of another fresh new day*
*- another new beginning*
*with yesterday washed away*

*Life is just a fleeting day*
*as death is just a night*
*as we pass through that darkness,*
*We'll be waiting heaven's light*

## Final Farewell

*Shed no tear when I am gone*
*- do not for me weep.*
*Show no sorrow o'er my grave*
*no somber vigil keep.*
*But wear a smile & gaily sing*
*- rejoice a time with me.*
*For now at last all pain is gone*
*now at last I'm free.*
*We shared together earthly time*
*- it meant so much to me.*
*But that was only briefly spent,*
*What of eternity?*
*Just put your trust in Jesus*
*and follow close behind.*
*We'll meet again in Heaven*
*-eternal joy to find.*

## In Memory

*I remember Daddy.*
*He always seemed so strong.*
*I remember Daddy.*
*He never could do wrong.*
*When I was just a little boy*
*he let me take his hand.*
*I'd hold onto one finger*
*and close by him I'd stand.*
*I followed in his footsteps;*
*they were so big and sure.*
*I followed in his footsteps;*
*no matter where they were.*
*I used to run behind his plow*
*and kick the clods of dirt.*
*But when I tripped or stubbed a toe,*
*I'd hide from him the hurt.*
*I often wondered how he knew*
*so many, many things.*
*And where he learned the silly songs*
*that just to me he'd sing.*
*I used to say "I'm just his slave."*
*when he'd make me work so hard;*
*but deep down in my heart I knew*
*he would never do me harm.*
*And often when I could have been*
*a whole lot closer done,*
*he'd come and help me with the chore*
*and even make it fun.*
*He never played at sports with me*
*or even parlor games.*

*But everything we did, it seemed,*
*was made fun all the same.*
*My daddy had a way with folks,*
*I never will forget.*
*He never did get mad at them,*
*but was friends with all he met.*
*He'd help just anybody-*
*They only had to ask,*
*and didn't even have to pay.*
*He'd smile at every task.*
*My Daddy could do anything,*
*from plant to fell a tree.*
*And how he knew so many things,*
*it still amazes me.*
*I helped him build some fences.*
*I helped him tear some down.*
*I helped him plant and harvest,*
*and haul the grain to town.*
*I often ran to meet him,*
*and carry his lunch box in.*
*He'd let me put his big hat on*
*and watch me with a grin.*
*He brought me bits of metal*
*from fact'ries where he went.*
*And in playing with this treasure*
*many pleasant hours were spent.*
*My Daddy was a Christian,*
*most anyone will tell.*
*He lived the way he knew was right*
*and taught it to me as well.*
*On every Sunday morning,*
*my Daddy woke us up,*
*and took us off to Sunday School*
*to fill our spiritual cup.*

*He gave me my first shotgun*
*and taught me how to shoot.*
*He helped me buy a motor car*
*and bought my gas to boot.*
*When I joined the navy,*
*my Daddy saw me off.*
*And when I came home later,*
*he met me sure enough.*
*He was always glad to see me.*
*He met me with a grin.*
*But I'm sure he never was as glad*
*as I was to see him.*
*He didn't leave great money*
*or land - or even fame;*
*but he taught me by example*
*to be proud of just my name.*
*'We have no greater treasure*
*than what we leave behind*
*in deed and reputation*
*of our name in other's minds...'*

*I said good-bye to Daddy*
*beside a wintry grave;*
*but when I get to heaven,*
*I know I'll see him wave.*
*There'll be no more sad parting*
*in heaven's peaceful land.*
*I'll follow in his footsteps*
*and take again his hand.*
*The mem'ries of my Daddy*
*- too numerous to pen..*
*We'll relive them one by one*
*o'er and o'er again*

Printed in the United States
By Bookmasters